Other Books by Tom Kingery

Think About These Things

Supplement Your Faith

You Need Milk Not Solid Food

We Rejoice in Our Suffering

Prince of Peace

The Letters of Jesus

The Ten Commandments Revisited

By His Wounds

Risen Indeed

Struck Down but Not Destroyed

The Better Part

Give Us This Day

Now Is The Acceptable Time

Resist The Devil

The Beatitudes: A Journey Home

Make Me An Instrument

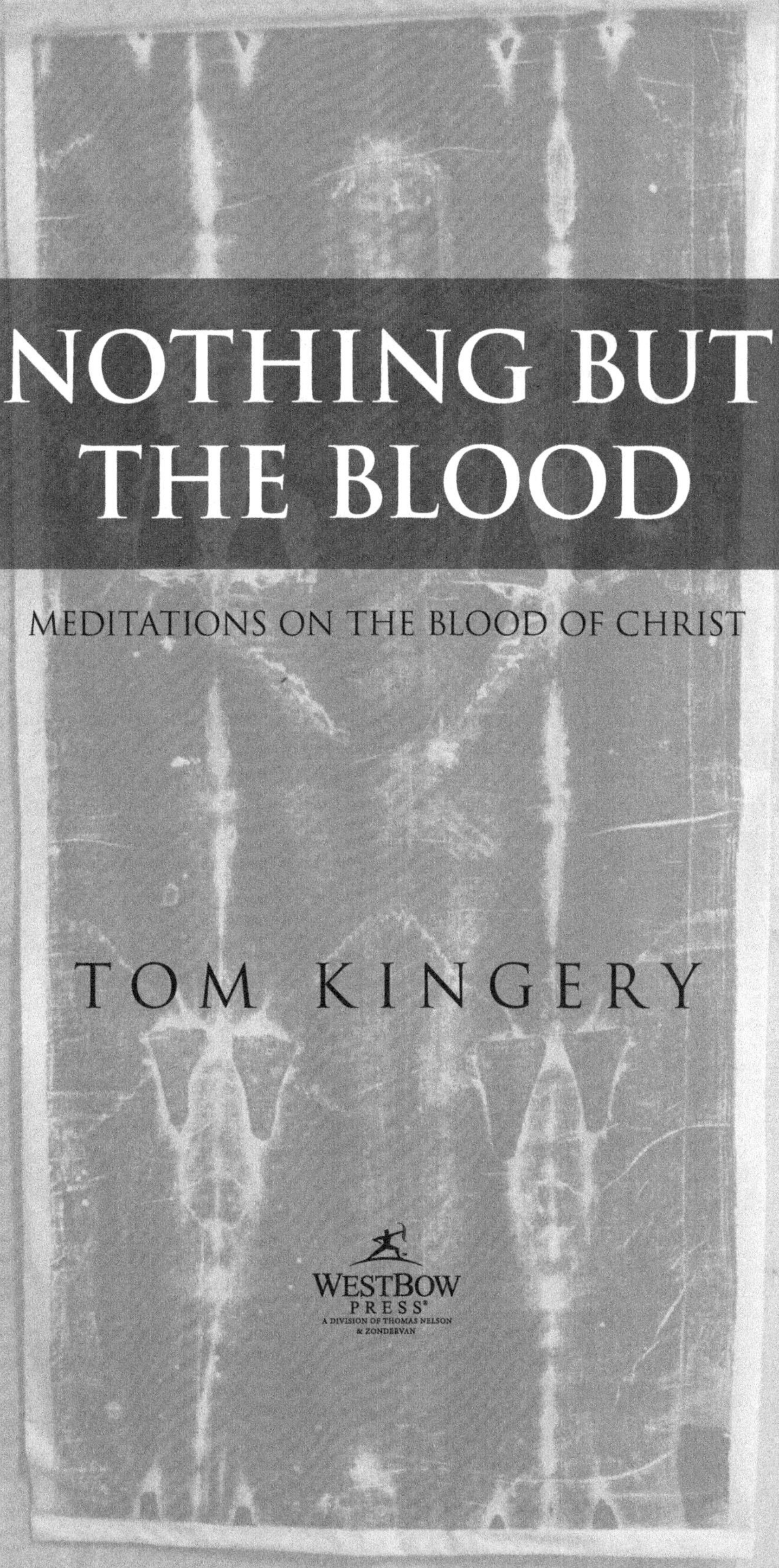

NOTHING BUT THE BLOOD

MEDITATIONS ON THE BLOOD OF CHRIST

TOM KINGERY

WESTBOW PRESS®
A DIVISION OF THOMAS NELSON & ZONDERVAN

WestBow Press books may be ordered through booksellers or by contacting:

WestBow Press
A Division of Thomas Nelson & Zondervan
1663 Liberty Drive
Bloomington, IN 47403
www.westbowpress.com
844-714-3454

ISBN: 979-8-3850-4145-9 (sc)
ISBN: 979-8-3850-4146-6 (e)

Library of Congress Control Number: 2024927684

Print information available on the last page.

WestBow Press rev. date: 01/07/2025

INTRODUCTION

He came out and went, as was his custom, to the Mount of Olives. And His the disciples followed him. When he reached the place, he said to them, "Pray that you may not come into the time of trial." Then he withdrew from them about a stone's throw, knelt down and prayed, "Father, if you are willing, remove this cup from me; yet, not my will but yours be done." Then an angel from heaven appeared to him and gave him strength. In his anguish, he prayed more earnestly, and his sweat became like great drops of blood falling down on the ground.

—Luke 22:39–44

A Story

While working at a zoo, a young man was bitten by a rare and poisonous snake. He was rushed to the hospital. It was a race against time. About an hour and a half away from there, a man who had a snake farm and whose blood had built up a tolerance to the venom was contacted. A helicopter would rush him to the hospital where the victim lay unconscious as his heart slowed down due to the effects of the venom. A transfusion was needed. He could only be saved by the blood of the other man. The cure was in his blood! A life was saved.

Another Story

It happened in Vietnam. Two boys who were brothers lived in a village that had been destroyed by the North Vietnamese Army. The older brother was found badly wounded when the Americans came in to occupy the territory after the Vietcong were finally driven out. He had lost a lot of blood. After he was stabilized at the mobile hospital, he was still not out of danger. Badly weakened by his loss of blood, his body was unable to recover without a transfusion. Because of his blood type, the usual serum was inadequate for his needs. His younger brother was checked. There was a match. Through a translator, the nine-year-old was told that his older brother would die unless he could receive a transfusion. He needed his younger brother's blood. "Would you be willing to give your blood to save your brother?"

A tear came to his eye. His older brother had been protecting him when he had been injured. "Yes," he said, "I will give my blood." There were smiles of relief all around. He was prepared. The transfusion began. It hurt, but he knew his blood would save his brother. After about ten minutes, the younger brother began to cry, sob, and moan. Concern was expressed. The nurse stroked the forehead of the young boy and tried to comfort him, but it was to no avail. The boy just didn't seem to understand.

Finally, the translator was brought in. Yes, the boy was asked what was wrong. Was he uncomfortable? Did it hurt? No, he was not in pain. He was just very sad. Why? "Because," he began, and but he couldn't go on. Finally, he asked, "When will I die?" Then it was explained more fully. He would not die. He was receiving serum that would sustain his life as his blood was going into the body of his brother. The crying stopped. At about that time, his brother awakened, and his strength returned. His life was saved. The young boy had loved his brother so much that he was willing to die for him. He simply believed that his blood would save his brother's life.

> You know that you were ransomed from the futile ways inherited from your fathers, not with perishable things such as silver and gold. but with the precious blood of Christ. (1 Peter 1:18–19)

> In him we have Redemption through the blood, the forgiveness of our trespasses, according to the riches of his grace which he lavished upon us. (Ephesians 1:7–8)

> To him who loves us and has freed us from our sins by his blood, and made us a kingdom of priests to his God and Father, to him be glory and dominion forever and ever. Amen. (Revelation 1:5–6)

I pray that no one feels uncomfortable hearing about the blood of Christ. In Hebrews 9:22, we are told, "Without the shedding of blood there is no forgiveness of sin." If there is no forgiveness, there is no salvation. Jesus made the atoning sacrifice that frees us from our fallen nature. Atonement means that He bled and died so we don't have to. Our cure is in His blood. And He began to bleed even before He was arrested. The agony of His prayers in the Garden of Gethsemane became so intense that He literally poured His heart out. Was it blood or sweat pouring out of Him? Was it as much as the amount of blood that flows from a gaping wound? We see the sweat of God, the blood of God, and the agony of Christ. But this was only the beginning.

This book includes the many instances when Jesus bled or when His blood touched something. In the Garden of Gethsemane, the ground received His blood. He was being poured out. I am reminded of the blood of Abel. God said to Cain, "What have you done? Listen, your brother's blood is crying out to me from the ground" (Genesis 4:10). As Jesus prayed at Gethsemane, did His Blood begin to cry out to God from the ground? Adam was formed from the dust (the ground) of the earth (see Genesis 2:7). Human blood somehow seems connected to the earth. We are *of* the earth. Our blood is *of* the earth. Even our blood can enrich the soil. The ground speaks of and through the life the earth offers. And the blood of Christ cried out from the ground at Gethsemane. Jesus was in anguish. His earthly form was suffering as His divine form was preparing. Jesus prayed for me and you.

He bled for me even before He was arrested. How precious is that blood! How glorious it is to meditate on this gift from Christ. Consider what the blood of Christ can mean and the agony He endured because of my sin and your sin.

The title of this book comes from a beautiful song by Robert Lowry, which honors Christ.

> What can wash away my sin?
> Nothing but the blood of Jesus!

Blood

Your blood brings oxygen and nutrients to all parts of your body. Without blood going to your brain, which needs the oxygen it brings, your brain would have problems. Every organ in your body needs the nutrients your blood can bring. Where does your blood get these nutrients? They come from food and drinks. During digestion, there is a breakdown of the chemicals in the food you eat. The blood gets those nutrients and carries them through your arteries and to the rest of your body. It's an amazing process. Your blood is moved through your arteries by the pumping of your heart. Still, without your blood, your body fails very fast, so keep your blood flowing!

Scriptures

Here are several passages of scripture to help us discover more about blood and especially, the blood of Christ:

> Just as I gave you the green plants; I give you everything. Only, you are not eat flesh with its life; that is, its blood. (Genesis 9:3–4)

> For the life of every creature—its blood is its life. (Leviticus 17:14)

> Only be sure that you do not eat the blood; for the blood is the life. (Deuteronomy 12:23)

> Abstain from what has been sacrificed to idols and from blood and from what is strangled and from fornication. (Acts 15:29)

Much more surely then, now that we have been justified by his blood, will we be saved through him from the wrath of God. (Romans 5:9)

In him we have redemption through his blood, the forgiveness of our trespasses. (Ephesians 1:7)

Through him God was pleased to reconcile to himself all things, whether on earth or in heaven, by making peace through the blood of his cross. (Colossians 1:20)

Without the shedding of blood there is no forgiveness of sins. (Hebrews 9:22)

We have confidence to enter the sanctuary by the blood of Jesus. (Hebrews 10:19)

Therefore Jesus also suffered outside the city gate in order to sanctify the people by his own blood. (Hebrews 13:12)

You know that you were ransomed from the futile ways inherited from your ancestors, not with perishable things like silver or gold, but with the precious blood of Christ. (1 Peter 1:18–19)

If we walk in the light as he himself is in the light, we have fellowship with one another, and the blood of Jesus his Son cleanses us from all sin. (1 John 1:7)

To him who freed us from our sins by his blood. (Revelation 1:5)

What to Do

- Realize that your blood can save a life.
- Consider how precious the blood of Christ is to you.

- Think about this: Jesus is God incarnate. How could He bleed?
- As Jesus prayed at Gethsemane, did His blood begin to cry out to God from the ground? What do you think?
- Sing "Nothing but the Blood of Jesus."
- Think about if you have ever been lightheaded. Why did it happen?
- "Making peace through the blood of his cross." How could blood make peace?

A Prayer

Almighty God,

You have made peace through the blood of the cross. I am ransomed from the consequences of my sins by the blood of Jesus Christ my Lord. And I am grateful that I have redemption through His blood. Make me know this blessed cleansing more and more as I meditate on the blood of Christ. Make me aware of how precious His blood must be and how blessed I am to have Jesus, who sacrificed Himself, bled for me, and brings me new life by His Spirit, in my heart. In Jesus's name, I pray, amen.

Your DNA Is in Your Blood

Your DNA is in your blood.
    It tells the story of your race,
Your family, your flower's bud.
    And all that's needed is a trace
To put beneath the microscope
    Of life, of Earth, of every eye,
And you're exposed to being's hope
    While all existence passes by.
So when you bleed, you tell a tale
    Of your journey like a map
That charts your course and sets your sails.
    It overcomes each earthly trap.
        And yet you're somehow always free
        To find your soul's own destiny!

CHAPTER 1

THE WHIP

Then Pilate took Jesus and had him flogged.
—JOHN 19:1

In the midst of His agony and as Jesus prayed so intensely in the Garden of Gethsemane that His sweat became like great drops of blood falling to the ground, a band of soldiers, who was guided by Judas, was approaching. In the Gospel of John, when the soldiers arrived, it says, "Jesus knowing all that was to befall him, came forward and said to them, 'Whom are you looking for?' They answered him, 'Jesus of Nazareth.' Jesus said to them, 'I am he'" (John 18:4–5). And it says that "they drew back and fell to the ground" (verse 6). Why did they display such a shocked reaction? Well, Jesus was soaked with sweat. He may have been either extremely flushed or extremely pale from sweating so much. In the light of their torches, did He look as though He was one of the walking dead? Or were they shocked simply because His surrender was so effortless? Or were they shocked to hear Him say words that were too holy to speak? If He spoke in Hebrew, the statement, "I am," is the very name of God—*Yahweh*. Or could it have been a combination of all these things?

After a brief scuffle, instigated by Simon Peter and halted by Jesus Himself, Jesus was seized, bound, taken to the high priest's house for a quick trial, and then led off to the praetorium and Pontius Pilate. There was no trip to Herod in the Gospel of John; that's only in Luke. It was almost as if Pilate was alone with Jesus. Pilate himself moved back and forth between Jesus and the Jews, as they were called in the Gospel of John. Pilate examined Jesus briefly by simply asking, "What have you done?"

He was told by Christ that his kingship was not of this world (see John 18:36). Pilate came close to accusing Jesus of trying to be a king. But Jesus said something very cryptic to Pilate: "You say that I am a king for this I was born and for this I have come into the world to bear witness to the truth. Everyone who is of the truth hears my voice."

At that, Pilate mockingly said, "What is truth?" (see John 18:37–38). You see, from Pilate's point of view, power was truth. The one who had the power possessed the truth. Jesus was a nobody as far as Pilate was concerned. The petty people of Jerusalem were nothing in a vassal state under the all-consuming power of mighty Rome. You and I know that the ultimate power actually resides in God, faith, and the truth that reveals the kingdom of God. But as far as Pilate was concerned, he was just being annoyed. Yet behind every cynical attitude that outwardly mocks the relevance of faith, the words of derision echo back their deeper sense. Soon enough, Pilate would hear in his own mind Jesus's words coming back to him as "What *is* truth?"

He told the Jews, "I find no crime in him." And Pilate tried to appeal to a custom, which had been apparently established and practiced by the Roman governor at previous Passovers, of releasing one prisoner in recognition of Pharaoh's release of the Hebrews after the first Passover. But Pilate had contempt for these people of faith. He infuriated them by asking if they would have him release for them "the king of the Jews." It was precisely because the Pharisees saw Jesus claiming to be their Anointed One, Messiah, or King that they so objected to Him. Pilate may have known about the popular favoritism Jesus had gained among the common people when He entered the holy city only the Sunday before. Perhaps it was to this that He was appealing. It was a frail effort at diplomacy because they asked for Barabbas instead. The reason they did this is another story altogether.

Next, Pilate had Jesus scourged. William Barclay says,

> When a man was scourged he was tied to a whipping post in such a way that his back was fully exposed. The lash was a long leather thong, studded at intervals with

> pellets of lead and sharpened pieces of bone. It literally tore a man's back into strips. Few remained conscious throughout the ordeal, and some died. And many went raving mad (Barclay). Now imagine a cat-o'-nine-tails, which were nine leather thongs woven together to make one whip.

Some scholars explain that a scourging was called forty lashes, but only thirty-nine were inflicted because it was claimed that forty would kill a man. The purpose was not death but punishment. Sometimes, because the process was so horrifying, two men with whips would alternate inflicting the blows, partly to expedite the torture but also so as not to wear out a single man. Some scholars have imagined the whip as having more than a single thong. If it was done by two men, the man tied to the whipping post would have no time to brace himself for the next blow. He would react to the oncoming blow by either bracing himself or by pulling away from the infliction of something so painful. Imagine not one or two whacks of a whip—each able to tear and lacerate the flesh to ribbons—but thirty-nine!

People stood back not only to give room to the floggers but also because of the blood that would splatter and the flesh that would occasionally fly off as it was torn away from the back by the blows of the whip. It turned a man's back into what would have looked like flailed, raw meat. The muscles were battered, bruised, and torn. It was more than just his skin that would have hurt; he felt agony in every lacerated muscle of his back. He would have ached beyond any back pain that we might imagine. Certainly, the men inflicting the punishment felt blood spattering them. The whips, when the scourging was done, would have been covered with blood. And of course, the bleeding would not have stopped when the scourging was complete. It would have flowed unchecked by the protective tissue of the skin, for it, too, would have been shredded into uselessness. I'm sorry for the gross depiction of this reality, but it happened. It happened to my Savior.

My Savior took this for me. It is sickening to think of what happened to Him, not only because of the excruciating pain He would have endured but also because He didn't deserve it. I did. You did. We did. Certainly, I would rather have taken the scourging than the everlasting fires of hell, but I will receive neither, and you won't either if you accept His suffering for your sin. His blood was shed. He felt the pain. He drew the curse upon Himself that we might be set free—free like Barabbas.

Blood

Blood loss can be very serious. When you are losing blood, your veins and arteries pull water from the tissues of the body to keep the blood vessels filled. This results in the blood being diluted and the percentage of red blood cells being reduced. You will become pale and lightheaded. There will be a shortness of breath, among other symptoms. But the more blood you lose, the harder your heart will have to beat. Your blood pressure will drop, and after about 40 percent of your blood is lost, you will black out. Many will black out before this point. But you are in danger.

Scriptures

Here are several passages of scripture to help us discover more about whipping and scourging.

> By his stripes we are healed. (Isaiah 53:5 NKJV)

> Know assuredly that the Lord your God will not continue to drive out these nations before you; but they shall be a snare and a trap for you, a scourge on your sides, and thorns in your eyes until you perish from the good land that the Lord your God has given you. (Joshua 23:13)

> My father disciplined you with whips, but I will discipline you with scorpions. (1 Kings 12:11)

> A whip for a horse, a bridle for a donkey, and a rod for the back of fools. (Proverbs 26:3)

> They will hand you over to the Gentiles to be mocked and flogged and crucified. (Matthew 20:19)

> As for yourselves, beware; for they will hand you over to councils and you will be beaten in synagogues; and you will stand before governors and kings because of me, as a testimony to them. (Mark 13:9)

> Making a whip of cords, he drove all of them out of the temple, both the sheep and cattle. (John 2:15)

> And when they had called in the apostles, they had them flogged. Then they ordered them not to speak in the name of Jesus, and let them go. As they left the council, they rejoiced that they were considered worthy to suffer dishonor for the sake of the name. (Acts 5:40–41)

> Three times I was beaten with rods. Once I received a stoning. (2 Corinthians 11:25)

> The Lord disciplines those whom he loves, and chastizes every child whom he accepts. (Hebrews 12:6)

What to Do

- How do you respond to Pilate's question, "What is truth?" (John 18:38)?
- What would you do if you saw someone taking a beating?
- Are you grossed out by the description of Christ's whipping? How do you take it? Does it make you wince a little?
- Try to imagine someone suffering in your place.
- Meditate on being whipped. What are your thoughts?

A Prayer

Dear Jesus, we know how much You suffered even before You bore Your cross. We want to believe Your scourging would have been enough. But the weight of the sins of the world must have needed every drop of

Your precious blood, every cell of Your human, life-sustaining substance must have been required to atone for, to make up for our evil; and because what happened to You was so evil, we feel pain in our hearts, knowing it is what we otherwise might deserve. And we thank You for taking our place at the whipping post. Give us grace to sin no more, if only to honor the blood You shed to make us whole. By Your Holy Spirit, we pray. Amen.

You Lash Out

You lash out with your ugly words.
    They always leave a mark.
It's like you used a wicked whip,
    Or you were like a shark.
I brace myself for another swish.
    I hold my breath and wince.
I hear the sound. It makes a hiss,
    And sparks ignite from a thousand flints.
Blood flows from my wounded heart.
    I hear again the painful sound.
There's agony that tears apart
    The woven fibers love had bound.

And every lash destroys the thought
That kindness brought and goodness taught.
But my silence is forever sweet.
My victory's your whip's defeat.

CHAPTER 2

THE CROWN OF THORNS

And the soldiers wove a crown of thorns and put it on his head.

—John 19:2

Jesus Christ is King. He shall reign forever and ever. His kingdom is not of this world, but He reigns over *my* life. All the kingdoms of this world will pass away, but His shall be an everlasting kingdom. A time will come when the kingdoms of this world will become the kingdoms of our Lord, and He shall reign forever and ever. And if He is, in fact, your King, He truly rules over your life, and you are subject to His will, you will live in His kingdom and in eternal life beyond this one. Life everlasting and abundant is life indeed.

Jesus preached about the kingdom of God. It is like a mustard seed. It is like a merchant in search of fine pearls. It is like treasure hidden in a field. It is like a little leaven. It is like a great net that gathers all kinds of fish. It should be the very thing that along with righteousness, we should seek first in our lives.

And it is like seeds spread by a sower. And some seed falls among the thorns, and the thorns choke the seeds when they begin to grow. The thorns are an enemy of the kingdom; they bring pain while God's kingdom brings peace. The thorns draw blood while God's kingdom brings healing. The thorns are problems to avoid while the kingdom is a promise to keep. The thorns are ugly, but God's kingdom is beautiful. The thorns are a sign of the imperfections of this world, but the kingdom of God is constantly penetrating into this world and leaving its traces of perfect joy, love, and grace. The thorns are not worth saving. They will be gathered and burned.

But in God's kingdom, Jesus Christ is the Savior who is gathering His followers, His Believers, and all who come to Him, after having prepared a place for them in His Father's house. He saves them. He seeks to save those who are lost. As for those who are to be citizens of God's kingdom, "You shall know them by their fruits! Are grapes gathered from thorns, or figs from thistles? So every sound tree bears good fruit, but the bad tree bears evil fruit" (Matthew 7:16–17).

In Hebrews, we are told,

> It is impossible to restore again to repentance those who have once been enlightened, and have tasted the heavenly gift, and have shared in the Holy Spirit, and have tasted the goodness of the word of God and the powers of the age to come and then have fallen away, since on their own they are crucifying again the Son of God, and are holding him up to contempt. Ground that drinks up the rain falling on it repeatedly, and that produces a crop useful to those for whom it is cultivated, receives a blessing from God; but if it produces thorns and thistles it is worthless, and on the verge of being cursed. It's end is to be burnt over. (Hebrews 6:4–8)

Thorns are a symbol of evil. And a crown of thorns was plaited and placed on our Savior's head. The skin of His brow was pierced. The hair of His temples, already matted with sweat, would now have become matted with blood. Sick and dizzy with pain after His scourging, He was mocked by a host of centurions. One of the men—I wonder if his fingers were pricked as he did it—wove a thorny branch of briars into a circle that resembling a crown and placed it on the head of Christ. And the stabbing of its points would have made Him wince. Blood may have easily trickled down His bowed head, over His eyebrows, and into His eyes, dimming His already-blurred vision by the pouring of His sweat. And the defiance of their contempt for Christ brings revulsion to my heart. *My* savior was mocked, and they laughed.

But humanity regards that dark, dirty scene, and it does not join in the laughter. Humanity falls silent and stands very still. Although we're unable to alter that hour of deepest disrespect, humankind looks with disdain on Christ's mockers, wishing to come to His aid. But we are paralyzed by the shock of such total disregard for our Savior. Humanity is a victim of the same shame He was suffering. While at the same time, humanity is propagating that suffering by its sin. For every sin that we commit is like a thorn in that crown. Every act of willful disobedience adds to the scorn of the beaten Redeemer. Every time we fail to correct evil, we mock the good. For every moment that passes and fails to proclaim the kingdom of God and the reign of Christ, a moment is spent twisting the branch again and shaping it into a crown as it pricks the fingers of humanity and delivers the needlelike thorns into the brow of God in Christ Jesus.

Consider this act of mockery. It doesn't end with the crown of thorns, but it is such a blatant show of disrespect that it hurts. Such mockery was routine in the treatment of criminals who were going to die soon. Their self-respect didn't matter to the cohort of soldiers. But if you have ever been mocked in any way, shape, or form, you know it can cut very deeply. To cut someone down is a way of not only insulting them but also belittling them. How have you been treated? How have you treated others?

Oh, how our worship is mockery when we claim no redemption for the world. Oh, how our prayers are scornful as we seek our own benefit in some shallow sense of wish fulfillment. Oh, how our lives reveal so great a disregard as to allow what our Savior endured to have little meaning for us. Oh, how sad it is.

For as the blood dripped into the eyes of Christ, He became blinded so that we might see the grace of His suffering. As the blood trickled into the ears of Christ, He became deafened so that we might hear the good news of His perfect kingdom. As the taste of His own blood reached His lips and tongue, He remained mute so that we might give voice to the love of God, which was revealed in the hour of Christ's substitution for us. What a glorious redemption we have. What a gracious Redeemer He is.

And humanity still looks on. But some with hearts that ache for the Master, whose conscience is pricked by the pain of the thorns, and whose compassionate sensibilities are sent surging by the horror of the scene are compelled to care for the beaten Man with love that would change it all, if only it could.

Our King cast off His divinity to bear the curse of sin. Our King left His throne to take the pain of the punishment for those who are here below. Our King did not count equality with God a thing to be grasped, but He set aside His crown of glory to wear the crown of thorns, to receive the scorn of shameful sin, and to be mocked by a world that respects nothing of true honor. Our King bore our disgrace. He was mercilessly humiliated to make us humble, abased to bring us dignity, reproached to bring us respectability, and bled to bring us mercy. The crown of thorns was a sight that Christ did *not* deserve. It brought blood from the head of Him who is our Head. It cut into His skin to mock His reign, kingdom, and love, but it evoked in us the desire to follow in His steps and a gratitude for the true crown He now wears as we crown Him Lord of all.

Think about the crown of thorns. Think about the King. Oh, what a wondrous love it is!

Blood

Our circulatory system is awesome. Every part of our bodies receives blood. The veins and arteries are a complex network, which is not only a delivery process but also a healing and strengthening process. Babies, as small as they are, have only a fraction of the blood an adult has (only about one cup). The amount of blood in a person's body depends on their size. A person who weighs about 150 to 180 pounds has a gallon to 1.5 gallons of blood. Blood is precious.

Scriptures

Here are several passages of scripture to help us discover more about thorns.

> And to the man he said, "Because you have listened to the voice of your wife, and have eaten of the tree about which I commanded you, 'You shall not eat of it,' cursed is the ground because of you, in toil you shall eat of it all the days of your life; thorns and thistles it shall bring

forth for you, and you shall eat the plants of the field." (Genesis 3:17–18)

Know assuredly that the Lord your God will not continue to drive out those nations before you; but they shall be a snare and a trap for you, a scourge on your sides, and thorns in your eyes, until you perish from this good land that the Lord your God has given you. (Joshua 23:13)

But the godless are all like thorns that are thrown away; for they cannot be picked up with the hand. (2 Samuel 23:6)

As a lily among brambles, so is my love among maidens. (Song of Solomon 2:2)

I will make it a waste; it shall not be pruned and it shall be overgrown with briars and thorns; I will also command the clouds that they rain no rain upon it. (Isaiah 5:6)

The light of Israel will become a fire, and his Holy One a flame; and it will burn and devour his thorns and brears in one day. (Isaiah 10:17)

For thus says the Lord to the people of Judah and to the inhabitants of Jerusalem: break up your fallow ground and do not sow among thorns. (Jeremiah 4:3)

But if it produces thorns and thistles, it is worthless and on the verge of being cursed; it's end is to be burned over. (Hebrews 6:8)

For each tree is known by its own fruit. Figs are not gathered from thorns, nor are grapes picked from a bramble bush. (Luke 6:44)

Some fell among thorns, and the thorns grew with it and choked it ... as for what fell among the thorns, these are

> the ones who hear but as they go on their way, they are choked by the cares and riches and pleasures of life, and their fruit does not mature. (Luke 8:7, 14)
>
> Therefore to keep me from being too elated, a thorn was giving me in the flesh, a messenger of Satan to torment me, to keep me from being too elated. Three times I appealed to the Lord about this, that it would leave me, but he said to me. "My grace is sufficient for you, for power is made perfect in weakness. (2 Corinthians 12:7–9)

What to Do

- Examine your life to see if there are any thorns in your flesh or days. Pray about and avoid them if you can.
- Think about how "the cares and riches and pleasures of life" can be like thorns, which can choke out the word of faith.
- Does Christ wear a crown in my life? Have you crowned Him Lord of all?
- What is the kingdom of God most like?
- By what fruits are you known?
- What blurs your vision? What clogs your ears? What makes you mute?
- How have you been mocked? Who has mocked you?
- How have you been disgraced? How have you been humiliated?

A Prayer

Oh, Almighty God,

You suffered scornful humiliation at the hands of men, who produced the evil fruit of Your suffering. We deserve that gross disregard, for You were innocent. We are guilty, yet You suffered. We are shameful; You are to be honored. We accept the love You have offered us. You sacrificed Yourself that we might be set free. You have given us a crown. Let us never, never take it for granted. We are enabled to love because You first loved us. Help us to see Your holy, perfect love and the things You suffered for our sakes. Help us to see it, Lord. In Jesus name, we pray, amen.

My Savior Wore a Crown of Thorns

My Savior wore a crown of thorns
    That I might wear a crown of glory.
He felt the pain that still adorns
    And blesses now the holy story
Of how He suffered for forgiveness
    And how I now can know His grace.
Come with me and find Him righteous,
    Who bled and died for every race.

See the blood upon His back
    And watch it drain upon His brow.
All this compensates my lack.
    How gladly I accept Him now.
Do not take His suffering lightly.
    Do not turn from what was done.
His sacrifice now shines more brightly
    Than every morning that's begun.

Contemplate the blood He shed,
The awe, the agony, and the dread.

CHAPTER 3

THE PURPLE ROBE

And they dressed him in a purple robe.

—John 19:2

Psalm 93 begins by proclaiming, "The Lord reigns; he is robed in majesty! The Lord is robed. He is girded with strength." In Psalm 104, it says, "Bless the Lord, O my soul! O Lord my God, thou art very great! Thou art clothed with honor and Majesty."

Jesus taught that we should never be anxious about clothing. In Matthew 6:28–30, it says,

> Consider the lilies of the field, how they grow; they neither toil nor spin, yet I tell you even Solomon and all His glory was not arrayed like one of these. But if God's so close the grass of the field, which today is alive and tomorrow is thrown into the oven, will he not much more clothe you, O men of little faith?"

Jesus even taught that if we see the naked, we should clothe them (see Matthew 25:36). And in the all-consuming vision of our faith, where the victory of Christ is pictured, it says,

> Then I saw the heavens open, and behold, a white horse! He who sat upon it is called Faithful and True, and in

> righteousness he judges and makes war. His eyes are like a flame of fire, and on his head are many diadems; and he has a name inscribed which no one knows but himself. He is clad in a robe dipped in blood, and the name by which he is called is "The Word of God". And the armies of heaven, arrayed in fine linen, white and pure, followed him on white horses. On his robe and on his thigh, he has a name inscribed: King of kings and Lord of lords. (Revelation 19:11–16)

White is the symbol of victory. But notice how the victorious King wears a robe dipped in (or sprinkled with) blood. In the Gospel of John, the soldiers array Jesus in a purple robe (see John 19:2). In Mark, it is described as a purple cloak (see 15:17). In Matthew, it is a scarlet robe (see 27:28). And in Luke, it is described as "glorious apparel" and is placed on Christ by Herod's soldiers (see 23:11).

In the splendor that my Lord shared with God before His incarnation, Jesus was clothed with honor and majesty (see Psalm 93:1). On the last day of His earthly life, Jesus was clothed with dishonor and shame. The robe covered the wounds of Christ's scourging. It would have soaked up some of the blood flowing from His wounded back. It may have been placed on Him to cover the nauseating hideousness of the bloody mass of flesh on His back. And as much as you or I would cringe, if we were sunburned, the moment we clothed ourselves, imagine the pain of a heavy robe drawn across those open sores. Jesus was made to feel again the chastisement that makes us whole and the painful stripes by which we are healed.

Where did they get this robe? Was it part of a previous criminal's clothing—one who had the wealth to afford such a robe? The Roman soldiers who carried out the crucifixions often divided up the last possessions of the accused, as was done with Christ's clothes. Did this robe come from an officer's or a ruler's closet, and they wouldn't miss it? So maybe, it had been stolen (or borrowed). Wherever it came from, it somehow represented the mock royalty of the Messiah.

And to add insult to injury, He is taunted and mockingly hailed as "king of the Jews" (John 19:3). And the soldiers slapped Him around. They punched Him. In both Matthew and Mark, they even spit on Him.

Meanwhile, Pilate, pretending to be a diplomat, came out to where the Jewish leaders were waiting and said that he found no crime in Jesus (see verse 4). Jesus was led out behind Pilate, wearing the crown of thorns and the purple robe. I imagine the contemptuous gesture that was performed by Pilate of pulling the collar of the robe down to expose Christ's bleeding wounds before the people as he said, "Behold the man" (John 19:5).

And all the more enraged, the chief priests and officers cried out, "Crucify him, crucify him!" (verse 6). By this time Pilate really had the crowd stirred up, and he said, "Take him yourself and crucify him, for I find no crime in him" (verse 6). But the bloodthirsty Jewish leaders appealed to their own laws (perhaps the first commandment of having no other gods). They said, "We have a law and by that law he ought to die, because he has made himself the son of God" (verse 7).

When Pilate heard that, it scared him. "Where are you from?" he asked Jesus (verse 9). Then frustrated by Jesus's silence, he told him that it was within his power to release Him or to have Him crucified (see verse 10). The mockery continued as a mockery of justice. Pilate was just a pawn in this picture. Jesus even told Pilate that the only power he had was from the institution of his office (see verse 11). He had no power in himself other than from the responsibility placed in his hands. He would not be at fault. Jesus said, "They who delivered me to you have the greater sin" (verse 11).

Upon this, Pilate sought to release Him. Somehow, he was convinced that Jesus did not deserve what was happening. But realize that Pilate had probably been in this position dozens of times. An accused man, who was scourged and beaten, would probably have been before him at this very spot—perhaps, even daily. They may have been too weak to say anything. If they had any strength at all, they would either cry for mercy or go into a fit of rage, both of which Pilate would have returned with contempt. But no one like Jesus had ever stood before him—clear minded, rational, and even relevant. He challenged Pilate's better sensibilities, did not whimpering, was not belligerent, but was only righteous and honest. His last attempt to release Jesus came perhaps as a last-ditch effort to *not* have to release Barabbas. But his effort in graciousness was met with the threat of blackmail: "If you release this man you are not Caesar's friend! Everyone who makes himself a king sets himself against Caesar!" (verse 12). That's a good point.

Pilate's last act in this scene was his final expression of contempt. He knew that it was a no-win situation, so as he sat on the formal seat of judgment, he said to the Jewish leaders, "Behold your king!" (verse 14). "Away with him! Away with him! Crucify him!" (v. 15) they cried. They were angry with Pilate for playing tit for tat in his contempt. They would never allow Pilate to get what he wanted in that fateful moment. One last time, he said, "Shall I crucify your king?" (verse 15). And with a final expression of disregard for Pilate's desire to show favor to Jesus and in an expression of apostasy (for the Jews were to have no king but God), these Jewish leaders were heard to say, "We have no King but Caesar!" (verse 15). At that, Pilate gave into the pressure. He handed Jesus over to be crucified.

Later while Jesus was suffering on the cross, the soldiers who were charged with the crucifixion—four men—took His garments and divided them. They only gambled for the seamless tunic Christ had worn (see verse 23–25). But who would want such bloody clothes? Had Jesus been wearing them at all? It is likely that they had been removed before the scourging and that they were not bloody at all. But what value could they possibly possess for these soldiers, who were ignorant of the power of the blood. They were only pawns, as was Pilate, in the purposes of God. What they did was more than just a matter of getting what they could from the condemned man. They were fulfilling images of prophecy. They remain unnamed, insignificant, and only examples of the indifference of the world to the suffering of criminals. Still somehow, it is possible to see in them a sense of having something to gain at Christ's expense. In that regard, they are us.

How indifferent we become to the blood of Christ when it is cold and matted in His garments after the cross has raised Him naked to the world as a condemned man. Today, we see Him robed in majesty, honor, power, and glory. But the reason we can see Him this way is because for one hour of His life, He was arrayed in a purple robe that covered His wounds.

How are you arrayed? We're to "put on the new nature" (Colossians 3:10).

> Put on, then, as God's chosen ones, holy and beloved, compassion, kindness, humility, meekness, and patience; bearing with one another; and if anyone has a complaint against another, forgiving each other. Just as your Lord has

> forgiven you, so you also must forgive. Above all clothe yourselves with love which binds everything together in perfect harmony; and let the peace of Christ rule in your hearts to which indeed you were called in the one body. And be thankful. Let the word of Christ dwell in you richly; teach and admonish one another in all wisdom; and with gratitude in your hearts sing psalms, hymns, and spiritual songs to God. And whatever you do, in word or deed, do everything in the name of the Lord Jesus, giving thanks to God the Father through him. (Colossians 3:12–17)

In Ephesians, we are told, "Put on the whole armor of God so that you may be able to stand against the wiles of the devil" (6:11).

> Stand therefore and fasten the belt of truth around your waist; and put on the breastplate of righteousness. As shoes for your feet, put on whatever will make you ready to proclaim the gospel of peace. With all these take the shield of faith with which you will be able to quench all the flaming arrows of the evil one. Take the helmet of salvation and the sword of the spirit, which is the word of God. (Ephesians 6:14–17)

Put on the power of Christ, and Christ will put a white robe, which has been washed in the blood of the Lamb, on you. You see, there is power in the blood!

Blood

There is power in *your* blood. Your blood receives nutrients from your small intestines. The human body is more complicated than I want to understand. But your bone marrow creates your blood cells. Your blood cells receive the nutrients your body needs from your intestines as they digest the food you have eaten, breaking it down to create what your system can use. Your spleen deals with blood cells that are no longer able to carry those nutrients. (They may last about 120 days while white blood cells last about six days.) And all the while, your liver filters your blood. It's amazing!

Scriptures

Here are several passages of scripture to help us discover more about robes and being robed or clothed.

> These are the vestments that they shall make: a breastpiece, an ephod, a robe, a checkered tunic, a turbin, and a sash. When they make these sacred vestments for your brother Aaron and his sons to serve me as priests, they shall use gold, blue, purple, and crimson yarns, and fine linen. You shall make the robe and the ephod all of blue … a golden bell and a pomegranate alternating all around the lower hem of the robe. (Exodus 28:4–5, 31, 34)

> I put on righteousness, and it clothed me; my justice was like a robe and a turban. (Job 29:14)

> I will greatly rejoice in the Lord, my whole being shall exalt in my God; for he has clothed me with the garments of salvation, he has covered me with the robe of righteousness; as a bridegroom decks himself with a garland and as a bride adorns herself with her jewels. (Isaiah 61:10)

> I was naked and you gave me clothing. (Matthew 25:36)

> Now, John was clothed with camel's hair, with a leather belt around his waist, and he ate locusts and wild honey. (Mark 1:6)

> The father said to his slaves, "Quickly bring out a robe—the best one—and put it on him; put a ring on his finger and sandals on his feet." (Luke 15:22)

There was a rich man who was dressed in purple and fine linen and who feasted sumptuously every day. (Luke 16:19)

And see, I am sending upon you what my father promised; so stay here in the city until you have been clothed with power from on high. (Luke 24:49)

Instead, put on the Lord Jesus Christ, and make no provisions for the flesh, to gratify its desires. (Romans 13:14)

As many of you as were baptized into Christ have clothed yourselves with Christ. (Galatians 3:27)

What to Do

- How serious are you about clothing? Some people *love* shopping for clothes. When does such an attitude become wrong?
- How do you feel about being naked? What minimal clothes do you feel OK wearing? Does it depend on the setting?
- How do you feel while seeing Christ adorned with the purple robe? Remember His wounds. What do you do when your skin is sore?
- What does it mean that Pilate "found no crime" in Jesus? How do you feel about the whole scene?
- Have you ever seen a mockery of justice? What stirs within you when you do?
- How may you have had something to gain at another's expense?
- How do you picture Christ right now? Is He robed in majesty?
- Put on the new nature.
- Put on the armor of God.
- Be clothed with power from on high.
- Put on a smile.

A Prayer

Oh, Lord,

You have called me to cast off my old nature and to put on a new nature. Help me to choose a robe of faith, righteousness, and love. Give me such zeal for Your way that my spiritual hopes will be visible even more than the clothes I wear. Because Jesus was mockingly arrayed with a purple robe on the day He died, let me be blessed by an outward and visible garment of joy and praise to make up for the evil He endured for my soul. This I pray, in Jesus's name, amen.

The Earth Is Arrayed in Splendor

It's not enough just to say
    That the earth is arrayed in splendor.
But its beauty has a perfect way
    Of moving our hearts, for its beauty is tender.
        And we have the fortune to pause and to see
        The wonderful ways that it sets our minds free.

And then it's a gift just to know
    How truly awesome creation can seem
When even a simple small petal can show
    What is revealed by the sun's softened gleam.
        And we can interpret the glorious way.
        There is something majestic in every new day.

The world puts on such an excellent robe.
And hey, even we are part of this globe.

CHAPTER 4

THE CROSS OF CHRIST

Carrying the cross by himself, he went out to what is called The Place of the Skull, which in Hebrew is called Golgotha.

—John 19:17

Let's begin with a collage of scripture passages.

> The son of man also came not to be served but to serve, and to give his life as a ransom for many. (Mark 10:45)
>
> In Christ God was reconciling the world to himself, not counting their trespasses against them, and entrusting to us the message of reconciliation. (2 Corinthians 5:19)
>
> We preach Christ crucified, a stumbling block to the Jews and folly to the Gentiles, but to those who are called, both Jews and Gentiles, Christ is the power of God and the wisdom of God. (1 Corinthians 1:23–24)
>
> When I came to you, brothers and sisters, I did not come proclaiming to you the testimony of God in lofty words or wisdom. For I decided to know nothing among you except Jesus Christ and him crucified. (1 Corinthians 2:1–2)

> Far be it for me to Glory except in the cross of our Lord Jesus, by which the world has been crucified to me, and I to the world. (Galatians 6:14)
>
> I have been crucified with Christ; it is no longer I who live, but Christ who lives in me; and the life I now live in the flesh I live by faith in the Son of God, who loved me and gave himself for me. (Galatians 2:20)
>
> If any man would come after me, let them deny themselves and take up a cross and follow me. (Matthew 16:24)
>
> In Jesus all the fullness of God was pleased to dwell, and through him to reconcile to himself all things, whether on earth or in heaven, making peace by the blood of his cross. (Colossians 1:19–20)
>
> Now is the judgment of this world, now shall the ruler of this world be cast out; and I, when I am lifted up from the earth, will draw all people to myself. (John 12:31–32)
>
> As Moses lifted up the serpent in the wilderness, so must the son of man be lifted up, that whoever believes in him may have eternal life. (John 3:14–15)

The cross is a symbol of power. There is power in our belief, for we believe that Jesus's death on the cross is our salvation. The cross is a symbol of belief because of our very dependence on what happened there for salvation. Each of us is able to say that the cross is a symbol of our deaths because Christ died for us. Each of us is able to say that the cross is a symbol of the death of my sins because the suffering and punishment Christ received was on behalf of my sins and the sins of the world. The cross is a symbol of death's defeat, for the cross is now empty and so is the grave.

The cross is a symbol of power over evil, as in the mythical image of it being used to chase away demons and defend against vampires. The cross is a symbol of the death of selfishness, as we are called in our discipleship to deny ourselves, to take up a cross, to follow the example of Christ, and to make sacrifices for the sake of others. The cross is the symbol of grace because Jesus gave His life to give us the free gift of forgiveness. The cross is a symbol of forgiveness and reconciliation because the cross was where Jesus ransomed us. The cross is a symbol of love because God so loved the world that He gave His only Son.

The cross is a symbol of judgment because they who believe in Jesus are not condemned; but those who do not believe are condemned already because they have not believed in the name of the only Son of God (see John 3:18). And the cross is a symbol of faith because of our trust in this grand act of reconciliation.

After being scourged and beaten, Jesus was then made to bear His cross or at least the crossbeam for it from the praetorium to Golgotha, the place of the skull. We often picture something almost the size of a railroad tie, which weighed a hundred pounds or so, but that is very unlikely. It would have been a waste of good lumber. More practical was a minimal board, which was only strong enough to hold a man's weight suspended indefinitely as he suffered.

The upright post would have been sturdier. And although I prefer to envision a fully made cross dragged up the Trail of Tears to Calvary outside the city walls, the Romans were far more practical than to stack whole crosses at the praetorium. And the impossibility of a beaten man carrying so much weight for such a great distance (two blocks or so) makes it reasonable to think that the post was already at the site of the execution.

The crossbeam would have been laid across Christ's wounded shoulders. It is likely that His arms would have been tied onto it as some portrayals depict. Matthew and Mark told us that the soldiers put Christ's own clothes on Him before they led Him out to be crucified. But nowhere do the gospels ever say that Jesus fell along the way. And in Matthew, Mark, and Luke, a man named Simon from Cyrene, a place in North Africa, was compelled to carry the cross for Christ. (In Mark, it is even explained that was the father of Alexander and Rufus). Did he get any blood on himself? I bet he did.

Certainly, the post of the cross would have become bloody. But that was where Jesus was stripped and was laid on His back on the wood. The pain would have been unbearable. Remember that His back had received the blows of thirty-nine lashes. The thongs of the whips had bits of lead and sharpened bones in their tails. His back had been ripped and shredded. Now the blood, if its flow had slowed, was pouring again. And it would get worse.

But the soldiers charged with this act of execution probably wouldn't have cared. Jesus was condemned to death. Some in the crowd who followed the way to Golgotha did care though. In Luke, a group of women bewailed and lamented Him (see Luke 23:27–31). But Jesus told them not to weep for Him.

> Weep for yourselves, and weep for your children, for behold the days are coming when they will say, "Blessed are the barren and the wombs that never bore and the breasts that never gave suck." Then they will begin to say to the mountains, "Fall on us," and to the hills, "Cover us," for if they do this when the wood is green, what will happen when it is dry?

If the fire of hell is consuming the best of the best, watch out for those who deserve the worst.

Where do you see yourself in this bloody scene? Are you willing to take up that cross and let some of the blood of Christ rub off on you? Are you just a spectator? Do you lament? Knowing what you know now, do you honor the excruciating pain your Savior suffered? Or do you think that Jesus was crucified on a brass-coated cross between two candles in a colorful, well-lit sanctuary?

Listen carefully. Hebrews 10:19–39 says,

> Therefore, my friends, since we have confidence to enter the sanctuary by the blood of Jesus, by the new and living way that he opened for us through the curtain (that is through his flesh), and since we have a great high priest over the house of God, let us approach with a true heart in full assurance of faith, with our hearts sprinkled clean from an evil conscience and our bodies washed with pure water. Let us hold fast to the confession of our hope without wavering, for he who has promised is faithful.

And let us consider how to provoke one another to love and good deeds, not neglecting to meet together, as is the habit of some, but encouraging one another, and all the more as you see the Day approaching. For if we willfully persist in sin after having received the knowledge of the truth, there no longer remains a sacrifice for sins, but a fearful prospect of judgment, and a fury of fire that will consume the adversaries. Anyone who has violated the law of Moses dies without mercy "on the testimony of two or three witnesses." How much worse punishment do you think will be deserved by those who have spurned the Son of God, profaned the blood of the covenant by which they were sanctified, and outraged the Spirit of Grace? For we know the one who said, "Vengeance is mine, I will repay." And again, "The Lord will judge his people." It is a fearful thing to fall into the hands of the living God. But recall those earlier days when, after you had been enlightened, you endured a hard struggle with sufferings, sometimes being publicly exposed to abuse and persecution, and sometimes being partners with those so treated. For you had compassion for those who were in prison, and you cheerfully accepted the plundering of your possessions, knowing that you yourselves possess something better and more lasting. Do not, therefore, abandon that confidence of yours; it brings a great reward. For you need endurance, so that when you have done the will of God, you may receive what was promised. For yet, "in a very little while, the one who is coming will come and will not delay; but my righteous one will live by faith. My soul takes no pleasure in anyone who shrinks back."

But we are not among those who shrink back and so are lost, but among those who have faith and so are saved. No! We do not "profane the blood of the covenant!" We do not take for granted the agony our Savior suffered for us. We do not sin deliberately knowing that Jesus already died for our

> sins. We would not be so contemptuous, for we are a part of a New Covenant in the blood of Jesus. O God, make us all the more part of Your covenant of grace. May we participate in the Blood of Christ as true partakers. Far be it from us to glory except in the cross of our Lord Jesus Christ, by which the world has been crucified to us, and we to the world.

BLOOD

There should be no doubt after this chapter that in a discourse like this one, I should definitely say something about the sacramental aspect of the blood of Christ. We remember His blood. We are called on to eat Jesus's flesh and to drink Jesus's blood through the symbols of the bread and the cup as we celebrate His last supper in the upper room. It's sort of gross to take it literally and not just symbolically, but we are receiving Jesus in a very special way. What do you remember?

SCRIPTURES

Here are several passages of scripture to help us discover more about the cross.

> I decided to know nothing among you except Jesus Christ, and him crucified. (1 Corinthians 2:2)

> All we like sheep have gone astray; we have all turned to our own way, and the Lord has laid on him the iniquity of us all. (Isaiah 53:6)

> Just as the Moses lifted up the serpent in the wilderness, so must the son of man be lifted up. (John 3:14)

> This man, handed over to you, according to the definite plan and foreknowledge of God, you crucified and killed by the hands of those outside the law. (Acts 2:23)

The God of our ancestors raised up Jesus, whom you had killed by hanging him on a tree. (Acts 5:30)

God proves his love for us in that while we were still sinners Christ died for us. (Romans 5:8)

For if we have been united with him in a death like his, we will certainly be united with him in a resurrection like his. We know that our old self was crucified with him so that the body of sin might be destroyed and we might no longer be enslaved to sin. (Romans 6:5–6)

The message about the cross is foolishness to those who are perishing, but to us who are being saved it is the power of God. (1 Corinthians 1:18)

Jews demand signs and Greeks desire wisdom, but we proclaim Christ crucified, a stumbling block to Jews and foolishness to Gentiles. (1 Corinthians 1:23)

Christ redeemed us from the curse of the law by becoming a curse for us—for it is written, "Cursed is everyone who hangs on a tree." (Galatians 3:13)

May I never boast of anything except the cross of our Lord Jesus Christ, by which the world has been crucified to me and I to the world. (Galatians 6:14)

Looking to Jesus the pioneer and perfecter of our faith, who for the sake of the joy that was set before us endured the cross, disregarding its shame, and has taken his seat at the right hand of the throne of God. (Hebrews 12:2)

He himself bore our sins in His body on the cross, so that, free from sins, we might live for righteousness; by his wounds you have been healed. (1 Peter 2:24)

What to Do

- "Consider yourselves dead to sin and alive to God in Christ Jesus" (Romans 6:11).
- Consider yourself reconciled to the Lord because God does not count your sins against you based on what Christ has done.
- Don't let the Crucifixion be a stumbling block. See it as the power and wisdom of God.
- Consider yourself to be crucified to the world.
- Think of how your belief makes this possible: I "have been crucified with Christ; it is no longer I who live, but Christ who lives in me" (Galatians 2:20).
- Think of all the ways that the symbols of the cross have been listed. Can you think of more ways that it is a symbol. Try to agree with the ways that are listed here.
- Think of the cinematic depictions of the cross that Jesus carried. What do you envision?
- Think of how some of Jesus's blood would have gotten on the cross.
- "If they do this when the wood is green, what will happen when it is dry?" What does this mean?
- Think of how you might have "confidence to enter the sanctuary by the blood of Jesus" (Hebrews 10:19).
- "Consider how to provoke one another to love and good deeds" (Hebrews 10:24).
- Do not take for granted the agony our Savior, who suffered for you.
- When you hear, "The blood of Christ," when it is mentioned during the sacrament of Communion, what should you remember?

A Prayer

Let this be our prayer. It is from Philippians 2:1–11.

> If there is any encouragement in Christ, any consolation from love, any sharing in the Spirit. any compassion and sympathy, make my joy complete; be of the same mind, having the same love, being in full accord and of one

mind. Do nothing from selfish ambition or conceit, but in humility regard others as better than yourselves. Let each of you look not to your own interests, but to the interest of others. Let the same mind be in you that was in Christ Jesus, who, though he was in the form of God, did not regard equality with God as something to be exploited, but emptied himself, taking the form of a slave, being born in human likeness. And being found in human form, he humbled himself and became obedient to the point of death—even death on a cross. Therefore God also highly exalted him and gave him the name that is above every name, so that at the name of Jesus every knee should bend in heaven and on earth and under the earth, and every tongue should confess that Jesus Christ is Lord, to the glory of God the father. Amen.

THE HUMILITY OF THE CROSS

The humility of the cross,
    Is a message for us all.
We all suffered the loss
    Of innocence in the fall.

Vanity and pride are always out of place.
    We need to find redemption
For our falseness and disgrace.
    There's really no exemption.

For Jesus is our ransom paid.
    His atonement sets us free.
Following in the way He made
    Helps us be what we should be.

        We are called on to believe it,
        And then we will receive it.

CHAPTER 5

THE NAILS

There they crucified him, and with him two others, one on either side, with Jesus between them. Pilare also had an inscription written and put on the cross. It read "Jesus of Nazareth, the king of the Jews." Many of the Jews read this inscription, because the place where Jesus was crucified was near the city; and it was written in Hebrew, and Latin, and in Greek. Then the Chief Priests of the Jews said to Pilate, "Do not write 'the King of the Jews', but, 'This man said, "I am the King of the Jews."'" Pilate answered, "What I have written I have written."

—John 19:18–22

Ray Boltz sings the song "The Hammer." It's about a Roman soldier who is outraged to see a man who has been crucified and who is dying on the cross. He doesn't understand until he turns and sees the hammer in *his* hand. And finally, he says, "I nailed him there with my sins and my transgressions." It's a powerful song, and I think we need to hear it again because Jesus was crucified for our sins.

It can be a very powerful thing to meditate on the crucifixion of Christ by injecting ourselves into the scene. More often than not, we perceive ourselves as bystanders, helplessly looking on. But Ray Boltz has helped generate a personal perspective by creating an image and first-person language so that we can discover that we, as individuals, are the crucifiers of Christ. He had to suffer for our sins in order to pay the price of our redemption. We may as well have hammered the nails that held Him to the cross. Just as harsh is the discovery that we might have been in the crowd saying, "Crucify Him!" We may have even handed Christ over to Pontius Pilate, the temple guards who bound Him in Gethsemane when He was arrested, or God forbid, the Pharisees who condemned Him, plotted to have Him arrested, and conspired to get rid of Him. Or could we have been Peter, who denied Him, or even Judas, who betrayed Him?

Meditating in this way can make it feel very personal. At least, it should. More often than not, today, we feel proud to have accepted Christ and His sacrifice for our sins. But how do we perceive *our* responsibilities for the need of that sacrifice, suffering, and punishment that we deserve? Has an innocent person ever taken responsibility for your mistakes? Christ took on Himself the sins that you committed; He took my sins too. I deserve what He received; you deserve what He endured. What a gracious gift we have received!

> While we were still weak, at the right time, Christ died for the ungodly (that's you and me), why, one will hardly die for a righteous man, though perhaps for a good man one will dare even to die. But God shows his love for us in that while we were yet sinners, Christ died for us. Since therefore we are now justified by his blood. much more shall we be saved by him from the wrath of God. (Romans 5:6–9)

You see, God hates sin. We were created to bring Him glory, but our self-indulgent self-interest brings Him shame. We have dishonored God by our lack of respect for His love, for His gracious providence, for His abundant mercy, and also, for His extraordinary grace. For He came in the flesh of Jesus Christ. He taught us His way and truth, and He died for our sins.

We live in the age of grace. We are raised in glory by our knowledge of the resurrection. The passage in Romans 5 goes on to say,

> For if, while we were enemies, we were reconciled to God by the death of his Son, much more, now that we are reconciled, shall we be saved by his life. Not only so, but we also rejoice in God through our Lord Jesus Christ, through whom we have now received our reconciliation. (verses 10–11)

Reconciliation means getting back together. God was the One who took the initiative in making up with us and who was offended. Keep reading.

> Therefore as sin came into the world through one man, and death through sin, and so death spread to all people because all people sinned. (Sin indeed was in the world before the law was given, but sin is not counted where there is no law). Yet death reigned from Adam to Moses, even over those whose sins were not like the transgression of Adam, who was a type of the one who was to come. But the free gift is not like the trespass. For if many died through one man's trespass, much more, has the grace of God, and the free gift, in the grace of that one man Jesus Christ abounded for many. And the free gift is not like the effect of that one man's sin. For the judgment following one trespass brought condemnation. but the free gift following many trespasses brings justification. (verses 12–16)

Justification means being set right. God is the One who sets us right. We can't do it ourselves. Again, God took the initiative.

> If because of one man's trespass, death reigned through that one man, much more will those who receive the abundance of grace in the free gift of righteousness reign in life through the one man Jesus Christ. Then as one man's trespass led to condemnation for all people, so one man's act of righteousness leads to acquittal and life for all men. For as by one man's disobedience many were made sinners, so by one man's obedience many will be made righteous. (verses 16–19)

It was one Man's act of righteousness and obedience. We are the benefactors of Christ's sacrificial act on the cross.

An article from the *Journal of the American Medical Association* published in 1986 and titled, "On the Physical Death of Jesus Christ," a pathologist, Gary L. Fanning MD, and a pastor worked together to describe the medical aspects of the torture of crucifixion.

Having condemned Christ to death, Pilate ordered him to be scourged and crucified. The practice of scourging, by law, proceeded every Roman execution. The condemned man (women, senators, and soldiers were exempt) was tied to a post after being stripped, and beaten with a small whip made of several thongs into the ends of which were woven small metal balls and shards of bone. The severity of the beating often determined how long the victim would live on the cross. In addition to the horrible pain, scourging produced blood loss that frequently caused shock, leaving the victim just short of death. Following the beating, the victim was mocked and taunted, and, accompanied by a Roman guard, made to carry the crossbar of his cross to the site of the crucifixion. Because Christ was unable to carry his own crossbar, it is highly probable that His scourging was especially brutal.

The practice of crucifixion was initially carried out on a tree or upright post. The Romans learned this practice from the Carthaginians, and perfected it as a means of slow, maximally painful torture and death. Having carried the crossbar to the site of the crucifixion, the victim was stripped of his clothing, thrown to the ground on his back, (newly and badly wounded already from the scourging), and his arms were fixed to the cross bar by nails driven through the wrists. The victim and crossbar were then lifted up by four soldiers, and the cross bar was attached to the upright post. The victim's feet were next attached to the Cross by bending the legs and nailing the feet to the front of the post.

Once crucified the victim might live for hours or days depending on his general condition, on the severity of the scourging, and on the disposition of the Roman soldiers. Death usually resulted from a combination of factors: blood loss from the scourging often left the victim near death as was the case with Jesus; crucifixion greatly upsets

> the balance of breathing making it almost impossible to exhale without great effort and unbearable pain. The mixture of shock and suffocation leads to fatal rhythms of the heart, most notably ventricular fibrillation, which is probably what led to the death of Jesus, and would explain the suddenness of his death on the cross. The soldiers would frequently break the victim's legs to hasten death and would almost routinely insert a spear into the right side of the chest aimed at the heart to guarantee that death had occurred before the victim was removed from the cross. If the family did not receive permission to have the body removed from the cross immediately after death, it might be left on the cross for days to be attacked by predatory animals and birds. Joseph of Arimathea obtained permission from Pilate to have Christ's body removed for entombment. But Pilate, amazed at the suddenness of Christ demise, would not give permission until the Centurion confirmed that death had occurred.

That's heavy. For a moment, just think of the puncture wounds caused by those nails. It makes me wince to think of the hammer pounding the nails through the wrists of Christ. If His arms had been strapped to the crossbeam, nails in the hands would have been adequate to prevent Him from slipping out of the bindings. Even if He had been able to do so, falling from the cross while His feet were still nailed would have caused them to become so badly wounded—perhaps, even His ankles so badly twisted—that He would never have been able to walk again. But because of the gravity of being suspended in an upright position—with His hands higher than His heart—His hands would have stopped bleeding nearly right away, but blood would have continued to drip from the wounds in His feet due to gravity.

In the hymn "When I Survey the Wondrous Cross," the blood of Christ is poetically referred to as "sorrow and love" flowing down.

> Did e're such love and sorrow meet,
> or thorns compose so rich a crown?

The nails in His feet supported His whole weight. The difficulty of exhaling in such a position would have made Him try to lift Himself up just enough to let air out, let alone to speak in sentences. Imagine putting your whole weight on the nails or possibly, a single nail in your feet. It is likely that His cross had a small platform to which His feet were nailed. They would have been nailed directly to the post, perhaps held in place by two men as another hammered the nail. Our Savior received this torture because of our sins. For almost two thousand years now, He has suffered for the sins of the world then and for the sins to come—yours and mine. That's a lot of sin. It was a lot of suffering. We are the guilty ones; He was innocent. We are imperfect, fallen, human flesh; He is the perfect divine incarnation of God. Only God taking that torture could make the difference for all time. And ever since that Friday so long ago, the world has been able to know the fullness of God's grace. Do you know it? Is it not amazing?

There's another song by Ray Boltz titled "Feel the Nails." In it, he asks the question, "Do you still feel the nails every time I fail?" And the song concludes with, "I never want to hurt you again!" Yes, let us do our best to never hurt Him again. Perhaps, if we could feel those nails just a little bit, we would really want to be His comfort and not His hurt. Think about the pain Jesus suffered for your sins. Can you feel it? If not, give thanks.

Blood

I get lots of needlesticks! I donate blood regularly. I can do so every eight weeks, one pint at a time. At the local blood bank, I am on their wall of fame. (That's what I call it.) They used to have all the names of people who had given a gallon or more listed. Now they have the names listed in a binder. (They ran out of wall space.) I am there for having given over thirty gallons. It's a process that takes about ten minutes once the blood begins to be drawn. It's not too painful; although you do have to have a needle in your arm. I'm always impressed that they can find the vein they need. They feel your arm, poke around, then know where to place the needle. The good news is that someone who may have lost a lot of blood, either through a surgical procedure or a wound, can receive that blood, and it helps them heal. It helps others when we donate blood.

Scriptures

Here are several passages of scripture to help us discover more about the nails or about being pierced.

> She put her hand to the tent peg, and her right hand to the workman's mallet; she struck Sisera a blow. she crushed his head, she shattered and pierced his temple. (Judges 5:26)
>
> And now my soul is poured out within me; days of affliction have taken hold of me; the night racks my bones, and the pain that gnaws me takes no rest. (Job 30:16–17)
>
> Dogs are all around; me a company of evildoers encircles me. My hands and feet have shriveled. (Psalm 22:16)
>
> O Lord, do not rebuke me in your anger, or discipline me in your wrath. For your arrows have sunken to me; your hand has come down on me. (Psalm 38:1–2)
>
> The sayings of the wise are like a goads, and like nails firmly fixed at the collected sayings that are given by one Shepherd. (Ecclesiastes 12:11)
>
> But he was wounded for our transgressions, crushed for our iniquities; upon him was the punishment that made us whole, and by his bruises we are healed. (Isaiah 53:5)
>
> And a sword will pierce your own soul too. (Luke 2:35)
>
> They will look upon the one whom they have pierced. (John 19:37)
>
> Unless I see the mark of the nails in his hands, and put my finger in the mark of the nails, and my hand in his side, I will not believe. (John 20:25)

He humbled himself and became obedient to the point of death—even death on a cross. (Philippians 2:8)

And when you were dead in trespasses and the uncircumcision of your flesh, God made you alive together with him, when he forgave all our trespasses, erasing the record that stood against us with its illegal demands. He set this aside, nailing it to the cross. (Colossians 2:13–14)

The love of money is the root of all kinds of evil; and in their eagerness to be rich, some have wandered away from faith and pierced themselves with many pains. (1 Timothy 6:10)

He himself bore our sins in his body on the cross, so that, free from sins, we might live for righteousness; by his wounds you have been healed. (1 Peter 2:24)

What to Do

- Imagine feeling nails pounded through your hands. Does it make you wince?
- Identify with the different characters in the crowd. Are you just a passerby? Are you one of the Centurions? Are you a taunter? How do you *want* to identify?
- Let the suffering of Jesus be made personal.
- Think about how we share some of the responsibility for the need of the Crucifixion.
- Remember that Jesus suffered for your sins.
- Think of some of the songs that trigger the anguish caused by the Crucifixion in you. I hear, "Were you there when they nailed Him to the tree," and I choke up a bit.
- Think about pain. How have you suffered?
- Think about and remember the blood of Christ. After reading these meditations, do you think differently of it?

A Prayer

Oh, Almighty God, Lord Jesus Christ,

We do not know how many blows of the hammer it took to nail You to the cross. We can't imagine how much You actually suffered on our behalves; but we know that You felt forsaken. Help us to appreciate the way You died while being a substitute for us, taking our places on the cross, and dying for our sins. Help us repay Your gracious act of redemption with true repentance and the sincere effort of letting Your Holy Spirit live in us, for we *are* crucified with Christ; it is no longer we who live, but it is Christ who lives in us—so be it, amen.

Your Voice Is a Hammer

Your voice is a hammer.
    Your words are like nails.
You're cutting me down
    With such fierce ugly wails.

I am already beaten
    By my anguish and guilt.
And the flower of my soul
    Is beginning to wilt.

Do you like causing sorrow?
    Do you like feeling hate?
Is my internal torment
    What you want as my fate?

    But you don't see how you torture me so.
    You're just not aware. You might not even know.

CHAPTER 6

THE SPEAR

When the soldiers had crucified Jesus, they took his clothes and divided them into four parts, one for each soldier. They also took his tunic (now the tunic was seamless woven in one piece from the top) so they said to one another, "Let us not tear it, but cast lots for it to see who will get it." This was to fulfill what the scripture says: "They divided my clothing among themselves, and, for my clothing they cast lots." And that is what the soldiers did. Meanwhile, standing near the cross of Jesus were his mother, and his mother's sister, Mary the wife of Clopas, and Mary Magdalene. When Jesus saw his mother and the disciple whom he loved standing beside her, he said to his mother, "Woman, here is your son." Then he said to the disciple, "Here is your mother." And from that hour the disciple took her into his own home. After this, when Jesus knew that all was now finished, he said (in order to fulfill scripture), "I am thirsty." A jar full of sour wine was standing there, so they put a sponge full of the wine on a branch of hyssop and held it to his mouth. When Jesus had received the wine, he said, "It is finished." Then he bowed his head and gave up his spirit. Since it was the day of preparation, the Jews did not want the bodies left on the cross during the Sabbath, especially because the Sabbath was a day of great solemnity. So they asked

> *Pilate to have the legs of the crucified men broken and the bodies removed. Then the soldiers came and broke the legs of the first and then the other who had been crucified with him, but when they came to Jesus and saw that he was already dead, they did not break the legs. Instead one of the soldiers pierced his side with a spear, and at once blood and water came out. (He who saw this has testified so that you may also believe; his testimony is true, and he knows that he tells the truth). These things occurred so that scripture might be fulfilled: "None of his bones shall be broken" and, again another passage of scripture says, "they will look on the one whom they have pierced."*
>
> —John 19:23–37

Jeremiah spoke in a prophecy about the coming day of the Lord.

> Thus says the Lord, who stretched out the heavens and founded the earth and formed the spirit of man within him, "Lo, I am about to make Jerusalem a cup of reeling to all the peoples round about … On that day, I will make Jerusalem a heavy stone for the peoples, all who lift it shall grievously hurt themselves … On that day, I will make the clans of Judah like a flaming torch among sheaves … On that day the Lord will put a shield about the inhabitants of Jerusalem so that the feeblest among them on that day shall be like David, and the House of David shall be like God, like the angel of the Lord, at their head … And I will pour out on the House of David and the inhabitants of Jerusalem a spirit of compassion and supplication, so that when they look on him whom they have pierced, they shall mourn for him as one mourns for an only child, and weep bitterly over him as one weeps over a firstborn." (Zechariah 12:1–10)

Look on Him. The one who has been pierced is Jesus! God pours upon us a spirit of compassion and prayer as we fix our eyes on the dead, crucified body of our Lord. Look on Him. What do you see? Do you see a defeated dreamer or a sacrificial lamb? Do you see the end of a life or a finished work? What was finished in the death of Christ? There we are able to see the birth of forgiveness. In the death of Christ, we are able to see the death of sin. In the death of Christ, we able to see God "making peace by the blood of his cross" (Colossians 1:20).

Isaiah proclaimed,

> Yet it was the will of the Lord to bruise him; he has put him to grief; when he makes himself an offering for sin, he shall see his offspring, he shall prolong his days. The will of the Lord shall prosper in his hand; he shall see the fruit of the travail of his soul and be satisfied. By his knowledge shall the righteous one, my servant, make many to be accounted righteous; and he shall bear their iniquities. Therefore I will divide him a portion among the great, and he shall divide the spoil with the strong; because he poured out his soul to death, and was numbered with the transgressors, yet he bore the sin of many, and made intercession for the transgressors. (Isaiah 53:10–12)

Look on Him whose suffering was total and realize that as He poured out His soul, He was filling *your* cup. As He bore our iniquities, He gained more than just a portion of glory. He became the Greatest of the great, King of kings, and the Lord of lords. Look on Him. As He offered Himself, He envisioned you: the church, the offspring of His gracious atonement, and the fruit of His travail. His days have been prolonged as the day of the Lord has echoed down through the centuries, as the will of God has prospered in His hand, and as we continue to do it.

Look on Him. Look on Him, whom they have pierced. Only in John is the piercing of Christ's side mentioned. In John, Jesus spoke His final words: "It is finished." Then it seems that He quietly bowed His head and gave up His Spirit (19:30). In the Gospel of John, you almost get the impression that His dying moment was hardly noticed.

Normally, the Romans left their victims on their crosses long after their deaths. If life lingered, the Romans left them hanging, day after day, in the heat of the sun, and in the cold of the night. They were tortured by thirst and by gnats and flies that crawled in and out of the welts of their wounds. Often these victims died in the raving madness that ensued.

On that Friday long ago, as the day was drawing to an end, the Jewish leaders expressed concern about the approaching Sabbath festival of the Passover. They wanted things to be tidied up a bit. The three crucified and dying or dead bodies wouldn't be proper. What hypocrites they were made out to be as John painted a portrait of the farce of their faith. Anyway, the soldiers began to finish their jobs with the gross and cruel method of taking their hammers and breaking the legs of the crucified men so as to detonate their systems with such a blast that the blow brought death. But when they came to Jesus, they noticed that He was already dead.

As the story is told in Matthew, Mark, and Luke, there is no doubt as to the exact moment of Jesus's death. It happened at about the ninth hour (see Matthew 27:46; Mark 15:34; and Luke 23:44) or 3:00 p.m. The sky had been dark since noon. Then Jesus cried out again with a loud voice and yielded up His Spirit (see Matthew 27:50 and Mark 15:37). Luke reports Jesus as saying, just before He died, "Father, into thy hands I commit my spirit" (23:46). In all three synoptic gospels, Jesus's moment of death was a very noticeable event. From Matthew, we read,

And behold the curtain of the temple was torn in two, from top to bottom; and the earth shook and the rocks split; the tombs were opened, and many bodies of the saints who had fallen asleep were raised. When the Centurion, and those who were with him keeping watch over Jesus, saw the earthquake and what took place, they were filled with awe, and said, "Truly, this man was the son of God!" (Mark 15:38–39 and Matthew 27:51, 54)

Luke says, "Certainly this man was innocent" (23:47). In John, however, the moment of Jesus's death was missed by the soldiers. But as the day was drawing to its end, they had to finish their day's task and dispose of the bodies. Jesus's legs did not need to be broken, but to ensure His death, one of them pierced His side with a spear. And in that moment and from that final wound, there flowed *blood* and *water*—communion and baptism. They are the covenants of forgiveness, cleansing grace, and new life. I can't say it better than when we sing,

"Rock of Ages cleft for me.
Let me hide myself in the.
Let the water and the blood
from thy wounded side which flowed
be of sin the double cure:
save from death and make me pure!

Although it cannot be confirmed, scholars speculate that the spear pierced Jesus's heart and that the blood left in His heart when it had stopped pumping became mingled with the fluid of the pericardium. It came forth as the spear was pulled back, tearing apart the heart of our Savior. I'm not sure how long it takes, but another thought is that in the course of time between His death and the piercing of His side, the blood of Jesus's heart began to separate into red and white blood cells. The white blood cells would have appeared as an almost clear liquid as it came from the wound in His side. Even so, what little blood was left in His body was completely drained. Jesus was dead.

Look on Him. Look on Him whom they have pierced. Jesus was dead. His body had no life. The One who by His nature, was truly God and truly human was no longer alive as a man; the flesh-and-blood human nature of our Savior, Jesus, was dead. But the holy word, the omnipotent God, and the divine nature of Christ, well, that's another story.

Blood

A lot of people receive whole blood. That's what I donate now. In the past, I have donated platelets. The process is much longer, but platelets help people with more special needs like blood cancer, blood disorders, autoimmune disorders, and more. It is called pheresis or apheresis. The needlestick is actually a catheter in the vein. Blood is drawn into a pheresis machine, where the blood is separated. The plasma and red blood cells are returned to the donor through the same needle. (I go back to when donors used to have a needle in each arm, and the blood parts that are not plates would be returned into the second arm.) And within four weeks, you can donate again. Again, it is a way of serving the needs of others. The body rebuilds its blood supply naturally, and there is really no risk in being a blood donor. I encourage it.

SCRIPTURES

Here are several passages of scripture to help us discover more about the spear, the sword, and being pierced.

> He drove out the man and at the east of the Garden of Eden he placed the cherubim and a sword flaming and turning to guard the way to the Tree of Life. (Genesis 3:24)

> But David said to the Philistines, "You come to me with sword and Spear and Javelin, but I come to you in the name of the Lord of hosts, the God of the armies of Israel, whom you have defied. This very day the Lord will deliver you into my hand, and I will strike you down and cut off your heads, and I will give the dead bodies of the Philistine army this very day to the birds of the air, and to the wild animals of the earth, so that all the earth may know that there is a God in Israel, and that all the assembly may know that the Lord does not save by sword and spear, for the battle is the Lord's and he will give you into our hand. (1 Samuel 17:45–47)

> Jonathan stripped himself from the robe that he was wearing and gave it to David, and his armor and even his sword and his bow and his belt. (1 Samuel 18:4)

> He makes war cease to the end of the earth; he breaks the bow and shatters the spear. He burns the shields with fire. (Psalm 46:9)

For the lips of a loose woman drip honey, and Her speech is smoother than oil; but in the end she is bitter as wormwood, sharp as a two-edged sword. (Proverbs 5:4)

Rash words are like sword thrusts but the tongue of the wise brings healing. (Proverbs 12:18)

He shall judge between the nations and shall arbitrate for many peoples; they shall beat their swords into plowshares, and their spears into pruning hooks. Nation shall not lift up sword against nation, neither shall they learn war anymore. (Isaiah 2:4)

I will have pity on the house of Judah, and I will save them by the Lord their God. I will not save them by bow, or by sword, or by war, or by horses, or by horse men. (Hosea 1:7)

I will make for you a covenant on that day with the wild animals the birds of the air and the creeping things of the ground; and I will abolish the bow, the sword, and war from the land, and I will make you lie down in safety. (Hosea 2:18)

Do not think that I have come to bring peace to the earth. I have not come to bring peace, but a sword. (Matthew 10:34)

Then Simon Peter, who had a sword, drew it, struck the High Priest's slave, and cut off his right ear. The slave's name was Malcus. Jesus said to Peter, "Put your sword back in its sheath. Am I not to drink the cup that the Father has given me?" (John 18:10)

Who will separate us from the love of Christ? Will hardship, or distress, or persecution, or famine, or nakedness, or peril, or sword? (Romans 8:35)

> Indeed, the word of God is living and active, sharper than any two-edged sword, piercing until it divides soul from spirit, joints from marrow; it is able to judge the thoughts and intentions of the heart. (Hebrews 4:12)

What to Do

- Donate clothes that you never wear.
- Think about who will take care of your family when you're gone.
- People talk about making bucket lists or a list of things to do before they kick the bucket. Think about what you would like to do. How will you become able to say, "It is finished"?
- Think about what would make a time of great solemnity for you.
- If you have ever seen a dead body, try to remember what you thought when you looked at them.
- Think about why the gospel accounts of the death of Jesus are different. How do we explain this?
- Donate blood if you can.
- The battle belongs to the Lord! Think about how God is our best defense.
- Think about this vision: "Nation shall not lift up sword against nation, neither shall they learn war anymore." How does this vision affect your life? What is your attitude toward war?
- Think about how "the word of God is living and active, sharper than any two-edged sword." What does this mean for you?

A Prayer

Almighty God,

We are faced with the horrible reality that in Jesus, You truly died. It leaves us reeling. We, too, must die someday, but in death, Jesus has led the way. Because He goes before us, let us trust that as we follow Him, our death will not be as heartbreaking as we might imagine if we have faith in His amazing grace. For we know He is the Lamb of God, who takes away the sin of the world. For this, we give great thanks. In Jesus's honor and with grateful hearts, we pray, amen.

Failures Pierce Just Like a Spear

Failures pierce just like a spear
When they are remembered here.
Some cut deeper than they should.
Some turn into something good.
Some thoughts haunt my weary mind,
As if they're somehow unconfined.
They don't stay buried the way I planned.
They come from out of nowhere, and
I can't suppress them easily
Because they're still part of me.
But they've never really had control
Over my eternal soul.
Just remember that you need
To call on God, and you'll be freed.

CONCLUSION

THE SHROUD

> They took the body of Jesus and wrapped it with spices in linen cloths, according to the burial custom of the Jews.
> —John 19:40

The burial cloth of Jesus, the Shroud of Turin, didn't appear publicly until 1354, when it was exhibited in Lirey, France. Although there is some testimony to its existence before then, this is the earliest popular documentation of the shroud. It was acquired by the House of Savoy in 1453 and was moved to Chambery, where a fire in the chapel damaged it. Later in 1578, the Savoys moved the shroud to Turin. The shroud became a possession of the Roman Catholic Church in 1983.

It was denounced as illegitimate as early as 1389, and many skeptics agree that it is a forgery. In 1898, a photographer named Secondo Pia produced the first photos of the shroud. When the negatives of the photo were examined, the image on the shroud became clearer.

Whether it is a linen cloth painted very meticulously or a forgery of some other kind, it portrays the image of a man (both front and back). There are reddish-brown stains that correlate to the wounds of someone who was crucified. I do not want to debate the legitimacy of this relic because I can imagine why it inspires people.

I can imagine the shroud being collected and kept secret by some of the early disciples. It was rarely mentioned, if at all, because it was too sacred an icon to show off. During the early years after the Resurrection, the testimony of eyewitnesses to the risen Lord were convincing enough.

I can imagine that at the moment of the Resurrection, there was a burst of energy that came from the body of the incarnation of God, which was strong enough to leave an image. I call to mind the brilliance that occurred during the Transfiguration of Christ. God is light (see 1 John 1:5).

However we might accept its validity, the shroud should never be substituted for a sincere belief in Jesus as the Son of God. The shroud does not save us. We are saved by faith alone. Having any form of proof diminishes true belief to some degree. Do not depend on some tangible proof for your intangible belief. It needs no proof. For me, the continued existence of the church is proof enough.

But we know from the scriptures that there was a shroud or a linen cloth that was used to cover Jesus's body before it was laid in the tomb. And obviously, this shroud would have been stained by the blood of Christ. Did Nicodemus and Joseph, who buried Jesus, get some blood on their hands? I can imagine it. Did some blood seep through the cloth and stain the rock-hewn tomb where Jesus was laid? I can imagine it. I can imagine drops of blood in the praetorium, on the Trail of Tears, and at Golgotha.

Meditating on all these things can be very inspiring. The whip and the crown of thorns were intentionally meant to cause some bleeding. The purple robe may not have caused more bleeding, but it got bloody. The wood of the cross got bloody. The nails caused more bleeding and so did the spear. As we think about these things, there is something that moves in our hearts and stirs our minds.

But as much as we can rejoice in the ways we are touched by it all, it should end there. We become witnesses. Now, we are more convinced than ever before. Now, our faith takes on a deeper dimension. Our belief becomes more steadfast, and our understanding becomes surer. Something within us stimulates, energizes, and spurs us on. We grow in the power of what we believe. And we rest on the solid ground of our assurance.

With Paul, I want to say, "I desired to know nothing among you except Jesus Christ and Him crucified" (1 Corinthians 2:2). I can agree that one of our first purposes is to proclaim Jesus as the Messiah, who was innocent but was crucified for the sins of the world. It does not seem like a very positive place to start, but it is of primary importance to the Christian faith. I think the Resurrection would be a more uplifting reality to proclaim, and it is. The suffering and death of Jesus Christ are very heavy; and I hope this book hasn't been too much of a downer for its readers. But when meditating on what happened in order to get to the resurrection of a dead Man, you need to understand something about the death of that Man, who was the incarnation of God. Our God suffered and sacrificed His Son to bring us redemption, reconciliation, atonement, and salvation. Making this sacrifice was very important because, "Without the shedding of blood, there is no forgiveness" (Hebrews 9:22). Think about that.

Blood

It may seem like a sacrifice to donate blood. It is definitely a sacrifice of time. But I see it as more of an offering. Although the needle stick is slightly painful, it feels good to help another person. Even though we may never know them, they will know that someone provided this helpful resource.

Scriptures

Here are a few passages of scripture to help us discover more about what a shroud is like and about the death and burial process. There are not many.

> By the sweat of your face you shall eat bread until you return to the ground; for out of it you were taken; you are dust into dust you shall return. (Genesis 3:19)

> And the dust returns to the earth as it was, and the breath returns to God who gave it. (Ecclesiastes 12:7)

> And he will destroy on this mountain the shroud that has been cast over all the peoples, the sheet that is spread over all nations. (Isaiah 25:7)

> When he had said this he cried with a loud voice, "Lazarus come out." The dead man came out, his hands in his feet bound with strips of cloth, and his face wrapped in a cloth. Jesus said to them, "Unbind him, and let him go." (John 11:43–44)

WHAT TO DO

- Consider the burial shroud of Jesus.
- Meditate on the blood of Christ. Does it deepen your faith as you do?
- Be inspired.
- Be a witness.

A PRAYER

Almighty God,

When we die, we are often buried in nice clothes or clothes that might help to define us. We want those who have passed to look like themselves. Help us to remember that our earthly form is just a shell. It will turn to dust. But our spirit will live on in Your presence. We are thankful for the opportunity to meditate on the blood of Christ. Let our hearts be moved to tell others what we understand. In Jesus's name, we pray, amen.

WHO WILL REMEMBER ME?

Hey, who will remember
Me after I'm gone?
Will I be forgotten
When my curtain is drawn?
Will there be any clues,
Or even a trace
That proves I existed
When I've left this place?
Does it make any sense,

Or is it just vanity,
To want to be marked
By some small legacy?

But all that I want is for my simple story
To tell about how my life gave God glory.

A Final Word

What can wash away my sin?
Nothing but the blood of Jesus!

Printed in the United States
by Baker & Taylor Publisher Services